love is

WHAT IT IS

---•---

SHIRLEY C. WHITE

Love Is What It Is. Copyright © by Shirley C. White.

All rights reserved. Printed in the United States of America.

No part of this book may be used or reproduced in any manner whatsoever without written permission except in the case of brief quotations embodied in critical articles and reviews.

For information, address DW Creative Publishers, 4261 E. University Dr. #30-355; Prosper, TX 75078.

DW Creative Publishers books may be purchased for business, educational, religious, or sales promotional use. For information, please email connect@dwcreativepublishers.com.

To connect with the author, Shirley C. White, visit www.LoveIsWhatItIs.com.

FIRST EDITION, 2022

Cover design + Interior design + Editing by: DW Creative Publishers

PRINT BOOK: 978-1-952605-24-6

EBOOK: 978-1-952605-25-3

PRAISE FOR "LOVE IS WHAT IT IS"

When I think of the phrase "love is what it is", I immediately hear Granddaddy (the late songbird of the South Bishop Daniel White) singing "Father, help your children...Jesus is love, He won't let you down, And I know He's mine. Forever. In my heart". Granddaddy was the epitome of a fathers love. He showed me what agape love was here on earth. I did not know it growing up, but the unconditional love he exemplified to me and everyone he came in contact with taught me how to love others, my husband and my children. Just like Jesus, he never let me down and will forever be in my heart.

All the best,
Raevyn Cotton

I knew the physical form of my grandfather, the late Bishop Daniel White, for only five years, so his words and actions towards me were limited, yet the embrace of his love has always been present. His staple phrase "love is what it is" (that would become the mantra of the ministry) exposes my grandfather's ethic of love. My grandfather was the essence of charm, and his words were often so lyrical that they could be placed within a melody. Yet, the phrase "love is what it is" reaches past melodious and charismatic linguistic constructions to something tactile. The phrase is not a cliché, nor does it reduce love to our modern understanding of "it is what it is." The phrase gestures to love being more than words or actions. Love is something that is felt. My grandfather's declaration of love allows us to witness what love is— a feeling not bound by a testimony nor material interactions. Pappy knew best that after words and deeds— love, must be, what it is. Might his love, a mirror of agape, be shown in the ways we make those around us feel.

J. W. Martin, M.Div.
Yale University, PhD Student

What does "Love is what it is" mean to me? I really believe both the Late Bishop Daniel White (Daddy) and Apostle Shirley White (Mom), had the spiritual revelation with manifestation of the Word of God. Love is what it is, was the demonstration of 1 Corinthian 13:1-13 in action. I believe during their ministry over the span of their lifetime they encountered many people, sons and daughters, enemies, congregations, family, friends, and communities where they had to apply this word of love while demonstrating its attributes. My dad firmly believed you could travel the world, hold many prestigious titles, have the best education money can buy, but have not love, patience, kindness, tolerance and understanding for others, you didn't have anything. Love is what it is exemplifies accepting people without judgement, speaking the truth in love, raising other's up instead of putting them down. Love is what it is, is having the capacity to see beyond the faults, and see the need. The legacy of "love is what it is" continues to live on through our spiritual mother Apostle Shirley White and I believe will continue to live in our hearts forever!

Sheila White Martin

Nothing is more power than unconditional love. God gave His only begotten Son, Jesus, who gave His life for the redemption of man. This was an expression of **"Love Is What It Is."** Love looked beyond faults and met a need that no other could do for themselves.

Bishop Daniel White often used two phrases, **"Who loves you baby?"** and **"Love Is What It Is."** These two expressions were more than just mere words, Bishop White's actions backed it up. It brought a change of attitude and new life into a situation that seemed hopeless. A new perspective and a breath of freshness through an encounter, that was life changing. Bishop Daniel White loved with everything that was in him and he did not withhold that pure form of love, agape, from those he met.

It took me a minute to figure out that life's greatest meaning is found in giving, not in getting. Through a simple prayer, "Lord, give me the attitude of Christ. I want to serve as Jesus did." The answer to that prayer was in the person and example of Bishop Daniel White. He met no stranger, and he served the least to the greatest of mankind. I'm fully persuaded that selfishness was not a badge anyone could pin on him. The cloak of love did clothe him.

Real ministry began and hope was restored, through love

and the action of another. When nothing else could help, love lifted me. Of a surety, **"Love Is What It Is!"**

Jhaki D.
Elder Jacqulyn A. Davis
Minister of Music
Love Center Ministries Worldwide

As I reflect over the years, there have been many moments and a vast number of experiences that could be classified as "Love Is What It Is" testimonial episodes. This narrative will only reflect a couple. The first is the transformational power of acceptance and the impartation of "the will" to accept the challenge and move forward. In 1979, during the first year of the Pastors of Bishop and Apostle White, that Bishop White stopped by the courthouse where I was working at that time and as we engaged in a conversation he said, "Son, there are some difficult days ahead, but I believe that if we stick together, we can achieve what we need to build the Kingdom. All we can do is 'love' the people." Even though, I did not fully understand where he was coming from, I was willing to accept the challenge to the best of my ability. This was the start of a great mentorship. From this time forward through good times, tough times, personal crisis, family crisis, etc., it was the "love" shown through Bishop and Apostle White and the Church Family that brought stability. "Love Is What It Is" that brought contentment in the midst of "unrest".

Bishop Robert L. Davis

Affectionately known as Uncle Danny, Daniel White, Jr., was a memorable Man of God who was sent back home from Brooklyn at the right time in my youth in the late 60s.

Uncle Danny stood in the gap in the absence of my father. He showed me what being a man looked like. His strong attention to his wife, children and family was infectious. He had a sense of humor when called me Joseppie, which means Joseph but in another language. He was courageous to move back to the South from up North. Home is where the heart is.

He and Aunt Shirley taught me how to drive using their burgundy Mustang on the dirt road in the Village, James City. He tried to teach me carpentry by allowing me to help him with home projects. Although, disinterested I still worked with him. It gave me the little know how I have to this day.

The bottom line is, he showed me the love of God as did my mom even when I didn't love me. His teaching, singing and preaching when I was young was seasoning for my mind and soul destined to do the right thing while making critical mistakes.

To God be the Glory for the things he has done.

Gone but never forgotten,
Joseph Patrick Credle (Nephew)

I was about six years old when I first recall meeting my Uncle Danny. He had just moved from New York to New Bern,

North Carolina, with his family. On the first day he arrived, he dropped off his youngest son at my kindergarten school. He came in, found me, and introduced us by saying, 'Marvin, this is your cousin, Tony. You take care of him you here.' And that started our best cousin-friends for life.

So, over the next seven years, Tony and I were ALWAYS together. I would be at their house or Tony would be at our house. Uncle Danny was like a father to me, as he was to most kids in the neighborhood. But I was able to stay overnight at his house, eat there, and be treated just like one of his blood sons. He would take Tony and I to work with him at the local TV station, to local churches, and to small construction jobs he would do around the neighborhood. We were his helpers.

Wherever he was, he was always singing, either a real song, or just teasing with a melody here and there. When he started his Gospel TV show, the first black man with his own show in Eastern North Carolina, maybe the entire state at that time, we looked up to him as a local TV star. He would have the entire family on his show annually for a Christmas special. It was awesome and he was awesome! I looked up to him, was inspired by him, and truly loved him like a father.

Then, years later, after he and his family moved to Florida, they continued to come to North Carolina to visit his mother, sisters, and other family and friends in the area. One day while visiting, he said we should start to have a real family reunion. He talked about it and how we should do it and how it would work every year. And as you would think, the White Family Reunion was born. So, he is also known as the father of the White Family Reunion, which had its first in 1989 and has been going ever since. Uncle Danny has impacted my life in so many ways. I listen to his album often and he will live forever live in my heart.

Nephew Marv Credle
(His sister, Rebecca's youngest son)

Table of Contents

Songbird of the South	1
All My Life	14
This Love Is for You	17
7 Days of Love Is What It Is	23
Love Is What It Is	29
Love is Honoring God	34
Love Lessons Learned	40
A Holy Nation in An Earthen Vessel	44
Frequently Asked Questions About Love	47
A Melody of Love Divine	50
About Apostle Shirley C. White	53

LOVE IS WHAT IT IS

Songbird of the South

The Old Testament often tells us the number of years people lived before they died. Daniel White, Jr., lived a full and blessed life for 67 years before he went to his eternal home.

His life was full of love, life, and faith in God. On the same day he left this earth, he taught Sunday School to a room of seniors and his lesson was about God's amazing grace and the deep expressions of love we should have for each other.

This momentous book is created in his honor. Let his life speak to your heart through these three principles he chose to live by:

1. Love each other
2. Honor your parents
3. Serve Jesus Christ forever

Physical challenges had taken a toll on his body, and, as a result, he did not shy away from telling people that he was not afraid to die. As his strength was waning, he could see death coming and was prepared to leave this earth and call heaven his home.

Our prayer is that this tribute book would motivate you to

live well, to enjoy serving Jesus with all your heart and soul, and to love everyone around you deeply, just as Christ loves us all. May we all live in such a way that when we leave this earth, our family and friends who we leave behind will know what real love looked like and felt like.

Daniel White, Jr., was not only characterized by his love for everyone around him, but he was also affectionately known as the "Songbird of the South." In 1999, he released a musical compilation of faith-filled songs titled *Get Ready*.

God anointed him with an amazing voice, and he was blessed to sing these songs across the South and on various radio stations. No matter the location, he chose to sing songs that were highly uplifting and totally meaningful to him.

Let me share with you what I feel his best expression of these songs were. As you read further, you will come to know why these songs meant so much to him. And, perhaps, may some of the lyrics speak to you in some way as well.

God Has Smiled on Me

God has smiled on me; He has set me free
God has smiled on me, He's been good to me
He woke me up early this morning, He started me on my way
I just want to take this time out to say, thank you for a brand new day.

I believe my late husband could sing this song in his sleep. This song was incredibly special to him. When he reminisced about the goodness of the Lord in his life, he always reflected on how God delivered him from anger the moment he accepted Jesus Christ as his personal Savior. After that time, his life was forever changed.

Growing up during a time of segregation and deep racism in America, he experience a lot of mistreatment and misdirected prejudice toward him as a young man in the United States Air Force and as he got older. After accepting Jesus as his Savior, he knew he could forgive those who had done him wrong and live in the freedom Christ offers.

Christ set him free and put a smile on his face. He sang about that freedom in this song.

Get Ready

You've heard the story of Noah, how he preaches a hundred and twenty years,
but the words he spoke to his people,
the people they didn't want to hear
So, the rain began to fall
Seemed never to stop
Rained so much until it reached the top
Then the doors were shut and the people they knocked

but it was too late because the doors were locked

Better get ready
Get Ready, you better get ready cause He's coming soon
Hear these words I'm saying, listen to this warning
Get Ready, Get Ready
Get Ready, you better get ready cause He's coming soon

Singing and speaking the gospel were his gifts from God. He loved this song because it spoke about heaven and what it would take to get there. For most preachers, that is the core of their message.

When he sung this song, he would sing with great conviction, warning people to "Get Ready" for the second coming of Jesus Christ. This song made many people think about getting saved and it may have even helped some people to actually make the same decision he made to accept Jesus as his Savior and then live his life telling everyone about the goodness of the Lord.

He Sent His Holy Spirit

He sent His Holy Spirit
St. John 14 says let not your heart be troubled,
You believe in God, believe also in me.
For in my Father's House are many mansions,

If it were not so, I would have told you.
I go to prepare a place for you and where I go you can come there too.
I'll send a comforter. It's the keeping power.
He sent His Holy Spirit
I will come again.

This song is one of my favorite songs because the Holy Spirit is very special to me. Thank God for sending the Holy Spirit because as Romans 15:13 tells us, it is by the power of the Holy Spirit that we abound in hope.

It is by the power of the Holy Spirit that we stayed married for 44 years and birthed our four children within five years. We would not have made it through many stressful times without the empowerment of the Spirit of God.

As a couple, we learned firsthand the strength of God that He provided through Jesus Christ. I am grateful every day that the Holy Spirit continues to be my comforter, guide, provider, and leader into all truth and into what God has predestined for our lives.

Prayer

Prayer's the way, prayer's the way to heaven,
Faith unlocks the door
After you find out how to get through

Who can ask for more

You don't need fine clothes to wear
A brand new car surely won't get you there
You need Jesus
You need Jesus, oh Jesus
I'm in need of prayer.

This song was always playing in the White household. It was without apology embedded in almost everything we did. If one of us had a headache, it was time to pray. If our children were arguing with each other, they had to pray as punishment. We had many times where we prayed as a family, and, of course, many more times when we had our private times of prayer.

As a young couple with children, it seemed we always needed a miracle, and our Heavenly Father was faithful to answer our prayers. It was through the power of prayer that the Lord spoke to us and gave us directions to move where He wanted our final home to reside.

Although we started out in New York and continued in North Carolina and God used our lives incredibly there, Florida was the place God wanted us to take up residence for many years. Through prayer many souls were added to the Kingdom of God.

This song reminds me of Luke 18:1, "And he spake a parable

unto them to this end, that men ought always to pray, and not to faint." Praying continually is one of the most important things we did back then and that I still do to this day.

Look For Me in Glory

Sometimes when my load gets so heavy, and my way seems as dark as night.
I'm going to keep on looking to Jesus 'till I win this, till I win this fight.
One day I'll take my wings and fly around in the air,
to that beautiful City, so bright and fair.
Look for me in glory, look for me in glory,
Just look for me in glory. I'll be there.

Danny, as some of us called him, always knew he was going to glory (Heaven) when he departed this earth. In this song, he invites us to not only look for him in heaven, but also not to worry about him when he passes. In Heaven, he would surely be there, and it would be a much better place than earth.

While it is always sad to lose a loved one, there is comfort in knowing where you will spend eternity. The confidence he displayed knowing without doubt or reservation that he was going to Heaven was amazing. I wish for everyone to know the joy of peace and certainty for their future existence.

Nobody Loves Me Like the Lord

You took me through the hard times of my life
When I didn't obey your will
You gave me another start
Nobody loves me like the Lord.

John 3:16 tells us, "For God so loved the world, that he gave his only begotten Son, that whosoever believeth in him should not perish, but have everlasting life." This song is such a true statement. There is nobody in all the world who can and does love us like the Lord does.

A giver of love himself, Daniel White, Jr., expressed true love by his actions. He had a supernatural spirit of love abiding in him. And while he had a lot of love to give to his family and friends, he understood that nobody loved him like Jesus did.

Many people were constantly expressing their love and appreciation for him, but the love he received from the Lord was an agape love no one could give him. He sung this song many times and when people heard it, they knew it came from a deep well of understanding and immense joy in the fact that experienced the highest form of level every day.

Anybody Here

Has anybody here seen my old friend Abraham?

Can you tell me where he's gone?
He freed a lot of people
But it seems the good die young
But I just looked around and he's gone

Has anybody here seen my old friend John?
Can you tell me where he's gone?
He freed a lot of people
But it seems the good die young
But I just looked around and he's gone

Has anybody here seen my old friend Martin?
Can you tell me where he's gone?
He freed a lot of people
But it seems the good die young
But I just looked around and he's gone

This song was originally recorded by Dion DiMucci in 1968 and serves as a tribute to the memory of Abraham Lincoln, Martin Luther King, Jr., and John F. Kennedy. Throughout this song we are reminded of the fleeting passage of life. One moment, someone we know and love is here, and the next moment, they are gone.

James 4:14 expressly reminds us "Whereas ye know not

what shall be on the morrow. For what is your life? It is even a vapour, that appeareth for a little time, and then vanisheth away." Living knowing that our lives are a vapor causes us to do much more than just living. It forces us to get a fixed hold of the things that matter, causes we stand for, and the people we love.

What a Wonderful World

I see trees of green, red roses too,
I see them bloom for me and for you
and I think to myself, what a wonderful world.

I see skies of blue, clouds of white,
the bright blessed days, the dark sacred nights
and I think to myself, what a wonderful world.

The colors of the rainbow, so pretty in the sky,
are also on the faces of people going by.
I see friends shaking hands, saying how do you do?
They're really saying, "I love you."

I hear babies crying, I watch them grow.
They'll learn more than I'll ever know.
And I think to myself. What a wonderful world,
Yes, I think to myself what a wonderful world.

Yes, Daniel White Jr., embraced the world as a wonderful place and he endeavored to make it a better place through his life and ministry. During some of his most difficult times of physical suffering, he opened his heart and expressed how green the trees were, how red the roses were, and what a wonderful world God had created.

Sometimes, when we are going through difficult seasons of life, it is important to take a step back and really see the things around us that we might not have seen before. It changes our perspective about ourselves, about God, about other people, and even about our challenging situations.

Oftentimes, I would find Danny sitting in his car by himself belting out songs to the Lord. Singing brought him so much joy and peace. A melody of deep and abiding joy existed deep in his heart, and it helped to carry him throughout his life. In every chance he got, he would bring to our attention the greatness and lovingkindness of God. He wanted everyone around him to know about God and about his lovely creation.

Psalm 8:3-4 reminds us, "When I consider thy heavens, the work of thy fingers, the moon and the stars, which thou hast ordained; What is man, that thou art mindful of him? and the son of man, that thou visitest him?"

Thank You

Thank You Lord.
Thank you, Lord, thank you Lord, thank you Lord.
I just want to thank you Lord.
Thank you, Lord, thank you Lord, thank you Lord.
I just want to thank you Lord.

Lord, you blessed me once in
Lord, you blessed me twice
When I sit down just to think about it
You've been blessing me all of the days of my life.

In every detail of his life, Danny gave God praise and thanks. He did not let a day go by in which he failed to remind someone around him of God's amazing goodness and incredible omnipotence. His experiences on earth were focused on salvation, his family and friends, and all of the people he came in contact with each day. He never met a stranger, and it was clear that a stranger never met him.

The words "Thank you, Lord" were very much like an anthem for him. It was the tapestry weaved throughout his life and the way he chose to interact with others. He learned to live in thankfulness even through hardships, pain, sickness, and disappointment. He would always sing, "Thank you, Lord, for all you have done for me."

Daniel White Jr's life was a lesson for all of us to learn to love better, give thanks, and rejoice in the Lord at all times. We are thankful to have experienced someone in our lives who modeled what it means to be a Christian and to dedicate one's life in service to loving and helping others. I am thankful to the Lord we are still alive to continue his ministry of love and life across the world and to present this tribute to those who knew and those who may only meet him in heaven.

All My Life by Bishop Daniel White, Jr.

This poem was written by the late Bishop Daniel White, Jr., and it speaks deeply of the Lord's existence and the overwhelming sense of peace that one receives as a result of knowing Him.

No one on this earth is nearer to us than the one who keeps us and is always with us. It is not possible for parents, siblings, or friends to always be with us at all times. But God who is constant and faithful is always with us. Daniel White, Jr., knew that God was the one holding him up and carrying him through life's challenges.

Psalm 121:5 reminds us, "The Lord is thy keeper: the Lord is thy shade upon thy right hand." Understanding our need to be kept and carried is key to everlasting and continuous dependence on God. When we lose sight of that fact, we are more prone to depression and giving in to weaknesses than we think. Danny always kept this thought in his mind: God is good, and he keeps me in his presence and hold me in his everlasting arms.

I had a dream one night and I came to a vast place.

I don't know for certain the exact location of this place, but I begin to sing, and when I did, it was the words that came From deep within. I couldn't finish the song at that time, It was so overwhelming because the words were my testimony.

All My Life, the Lord has been good to me.
And there's never been a time He didn't bring me through.
For my very existence to this present time,
God has been good to me.
God has really been good.

All my life, Lord, you've been good,
Down through the years, Lord, you never left me alone.
God has really been good, God has really been good,
All my life and down through the years, God has really been good.

You touched the hearts of people, my family and friends,
To love me with a love that seems to never end.
The same God who has enabled me down through the years,
Is the same God who helps me to go now.

No matter what I've been through,
God's been with me all the time.
Whether I was up or down, on top,
Under or going round and round.

The same God that has kept me down through the years,
Is the same God who's keeping me right now.

This Love Is for You

The blood of Jesus Christ is God's ultimate expression of love for us. John 3:16 tells us, "For God so loved the world, that he gave his only begotten Son, that whosoever believeth in him should not perish, but have everlasting life."

Have you ever sat down to really think about and meditate on the love of God? Do you really understand how far it reaches, how deep it stretches, and how long it runs? Even when we are not our best selves or having our best days, the love of Jesus Christ sticks with us and if we allow it, it can live within us.

John 15:13 states, "Greater love hath no man than this, that a man lay down his life for his friends." Love in the world of God goes far beyond anything the world has to offer. It is the love parents have for their children but on a scale that is 100x more than that. This perfect and unadulterated love shown by Jesus Christ is what he want us to extend into the lives of our brothers and sisters, husbands and wives, parents and children, employers and employees today.

The blood and love of Jesus Christ speaks into your

circumstances and even into your place of work. Love gives you favor. It restores your soul and peace of mind. It helps you to receive grace and give grace.

In times of danger, love gives you protection. When you are sick, love gives you healing and wholeness. Love forgives sin. Love transforms our lives. Love paid the price for our freedom. First Corinthians 6:20 reminds us, "For ye are bought with a price: therefore glorify God in your body, and in your spirit, which are God's."

This price was paid not just with today in mind for every day of our lives. Everything God planned and allowed to take place at Calvary was for you! If he were here today, this is the message Daniel White, Jr., would share with you: God is love. There is no getting away from it or going around it. You will never find a love like Christ's to match. He cannot be outdone. On the cross, he wept, died and rose again just for us.

The gifts God has given us were given by love and should be operated in by love for God and others. God's love in me helps me to love the unlovable. The Spirit of God is love, it is not a natural, earthly love like phileo or eros, but it is a spiritual love that descends straight from God and is finds us right where we are and evolves us into someone better.

Galatians 5:22-23 tells us, "But the fruit of the Spirit is love, joy, peace, longsuffering, gentleness, goodness, faith,

Meekness, temperance: against such there is no law." When the Spirit of God is at work in us, we become amazing people. We look beyond the faults and offences of others and meet their deepest needs. We give ourselves away for the profit of more souls being added to the Kingdom of God.

Everyone longs to be loved unconditionally. Our Heavenly Father wants us to really feel love from Him and from others. Some people refer to love as "butterflies in the stomach." Others think of love as "a strong feeling." Still others define love through actions and gifts. God wants us to experience a GREATER LOVE that transcends human emotions. First John 4:16 tells us, "And we have known and believed the love that God hath to us. God is love; and he that dwelleth in love dwelleth in God, and God in him."

God's love is a love we do not often comprehend—a love that one would die on the cross for another. Many people go through life receiving very little human love. However, God desires every human to experience His love in ways that are often unexplainable. Love is what it is and to not understand and know how to receive and give love unexpectedly and inexplicably leaves a gap in our lives.

First John 4:8 tells us, "He that loveth not knoweth not God; for God is love." The purest and highest form of love is God's divine love that He offers to all of us. Love is God's nature, and it helps to inform us who we are to become.

We learn about love from God who is love personified. To be like God, our hearts must be transformed by love and our actions and decisions must be guided by love.

Love Center Ministries, the name of our church, received its name from the late Bishop Daniel White, Jr., because he showed love to everyone. His character was defined by love. He hugged everyone he met, and it made people feel welcome, seen, centered, and liberated.

Love Center Ministries taught us a whole new level of love from the greatest commandment given in Scripture. Matthew 22:37-39 states, "Jesus said unto him, Thou shalt love the Lord thy God with all thy heart, and with all thy soul, and with all thy mind. This is the first and great commandment. And the second is like unto it, Thou shalt love thy neighbour as thyself."

Luke 10:30-37 aptly describes a story that reminds us of our duty to be neighborly and kindhearted to everyone we meet, regardless of race, nationality, or social class.

> *"And Jesus answering said, A certain man went down from Jerusalem to Jericho, and fell among thieves, which stripped him of his raiment, and wounded him, and departed, leaving him half dead.*
>
> *And by chance there came down a certain priest that way: and when he saw him, he passed by on the other side.*

And likewise a Levite, when he was at the place, came and looked on him, and passed by on the other side.

But a certain Samaritan, as he journeyed, came where he was: and when he saw him, he had compassion on him,

And went to him, and bound up his wounds, pouring in oil and wine, and set him on his own beast, and brought him to an inn, and took care of him.

And on the morrow when he departed, he took out two pence, and gave them to the host, and said unto him, Take care of him; and whatsoever thou spendest more, when I come again, I will repay thee.

Which now of these three, thinkest thou, was neighbour unto him that fell among the thieves?

And he said, He that shewed mercy on him. Then said Jesus unto him, Go, and do thou likewise."

As we study the Bible, we can take notice that God's love has more to do with what we do than what we think or feel. Love is a choice, and it is one that we have to make every day. Jesus chose to go to the cross for us. He chose to bear our burdens, our sin, our guilt, and our shame. He could have backed out and gave up and told the Heavenly Father that he didn't want to walk this cruel path. But he didn't, instead Luke 22:42 tells us Jesus said, "Father, if thou be willing, remove this cup from me: nevertheless not my will, but thine, be done."

Are we willing to say the same thing? Do we lay all of our reservations on the altar and tell God that it's not our will that we want to do, instead it is His will that we want to accomplish? This is the type of love that draws us further away from selfishness and a mentality that is me-focused and puts us in an elevated category that chooses to lay ourselves on the altar and put others ahead of us to accomplish God's will.

7 Days of Love Is What It Is

The love that God gives us should never run out in our lives and hearts for Him or for the people around us. If you struggle to love or feel like your loving ways and expressions have been lacking, there is a way to get that back.

In this chapter, we want to dive into a full week of ways you can meditate on and take action towards becoming a more loving person.

Sunday

This is typically a day for us to congregate, worship together, and fellowship with God's children. Some may have just come through a difficult work week or struggling with family, but this day allows us all to assemble together and collectively receive revelation and inspiration from the Word of God.

The week ahead will come with its challenges. While there are battles that await us, there are also tremendous blessings in front of us that we must choose to also acknowledge.

LOVE IS WHAT IT IS

The one thing we should acknowledge and reflect on daily in our lives is that God is Love. He loves us unconditionally and regardless of the circumstances.

Monday

Monday is typically the first start to the week, and you have likely heard about the "Monday blues" as some people call it. Well, Monday doesn't have to be so blue and boring.

Because of God's abiding and everlasting love for us we can face any issue or challenge that life throws our way including difficult Monday mornings. We remain steadfast in the love God has bestowed upon us and we carry into our places of work with anticipation of what God can do in our lives and in the lives of others.

Go into work reflecting on the love of God and with your hope and assurance steady in his promises.

Tuesday

First Corinthians 13:4 tells us, "Charity suffereth long, and is kind; charity envieth not; charity vaunteth not itself, is not puffed up,"

In the Greek language, the word "suffer" means "to undergo hardship that befalls one, an enduring deep emotion, like agony." This is reflective of the experience of Jesus Christ when he went to the cross.

Preparing us to know the Lord better now and forever in glory, Romans 8:18 states, "For I reckon that the sufferings of this present time are not worthy to be compared with the glory which shall be revealed in us."

Love is patient. This agape love suffers all our weaknesses and burdens. You will know when love has become patient in your life when you are displaying longsuffering or endure difficulty and inconvenience without complaint.

Longsuffering can be a tough characteristic to comprehend, but if we work at it, it will produce great dividends for a long time. You cannot be a truly compassionate and loving Christian without the healthy fruit of patience. Patience is measured by our ability to endure something we would rather not have to deal with.

We suffer long and express love in our lives when we surrender our desires to help bring to pass someone else's desire.

WEDNESDAY

Psalms 136:1 tells us, "O give thanks unto the Lord; for he is good: for his mercy endureth for ever." Today is a day for adamant and exuberant praise and worship of the Heavenly Father. On this day, we ask him for nothing. Instead, we thank him for all he has done.

First John 4:19 reminds us, "We love HIM, because HE first loved us." We show our love by thanksgiving and by being good citizens of the Kingdom here on earth.

Thursday

We share God's love with others by the way we live but also by what we say, how we say it, and how we treat our spouses, children, parents, friends, and coworkers.

First John 4:7-8 states, "Beloved, let us love one another: for love is of God; and every one that loveth is born of God, and knoweth God. He that loveth not knoweth not God; for God is love."

Show acts of kindness, share your testimonies, talk about your struggles, and invest in the lives of other people. If we each aimed to reach someone else with the knowledge and love of Jesus Christ, the world would be a better place.

Friday

The Bible admonishes us many times to show compassion to others. Colossians 3:12-13 states, "Put on therefore, as the elect of God, holy and beloved, bowels of mercies, kindness, humbleness of mind, meekness, longsuffering; Forbearing one another, and forgiving one another, if any man have a quarrel against any: even as Christ forgave you, so also do ye."

Embrace those who are hurting with God's love. The compassion Jesus showed toward people led to some of the most outstanding miracles in the Bible. Let our lives reflect that same compassion Jesus showed when he walked the earth and when he went to the cross.

Let our compassion for people be shown through our love for God and through our actions towards others.

Saturday

What are some ways we can show God's love in our everyday lives? Here are a few ideas to get you started on your journey.

- Be generous to others
- Treat someone to a meal
- Send an encouraging note
- Give away some of your gently used clothes
- Help a college student
- Share your presence with someone, rather than presents

Beyond this week, take these challenges into future weeks. Let your daily life reflect the love of Jesus Christ. Each week, challenge yourself to do one thing that will help you grow in Christ's love. You will be amazed at the transformation and others around will be glad you did.

Love Is What It Is

Daniel White, Jr., would be the first to tell you that he never knew unconditional love existed before he met Jesus Christ. To be honest, I did not either. While my parents loved me, nobody really loved me like the Lord.

When I finally fixed my eyes on Jesus, I experienced real and true love without shame or embarrassment, without having to fix myself to look better than I was. Jesus accepted me just as I was and we also ought to accept others just as they are, without judgment and without trying to fix them into the likeness of who we want them to be.

A list of words taken from 1 Corinthians 13 describes godly love as agape. This type of love is:

- Patient
- Kind
- Does not envy
- Does not boast
- Is not proud

- Does not dishonor others
- Is not self-seeking
- Is not easily angered
- Keeps no record of wrongs

First Corinthians 13 reads like this:

> "Though I speak with the tongues of men and of angels, and have not charity, I am become as sounding brass, or a tinkling cymbal.
>
> And though I have the gift of prophecy, and understand all mysteries, and all knowledge; and though I have all faith, so that I could remove mountains, and have not charity, I am nothing.
>
> And though I bestow all my goods to feed the poor, and though I give my body to be burned, and have not charity, it profiteth me nothing.
>
> Charity suffereth long, and is kind; charity envieth not; charity vaunteth not itself, is not puffed up,
>
> Doth not behave itself unseemly, seeketh not her own, is not easily provoked, thinketh no evil;
>
> Rejoiceth not in iniquity, but rejoiceth in the truth;
>
> Beareth all things, believeth all things, hopeth all

things, endureth all things.

Charity never faileth: but whether there be prophecies, they shall fail; whether there be tongues, they shall cease; whether there be knowledge, it shall vanish away.

For we know in part, and we prophesy in part.

But when that which is perfect is come, then that which is in part shall be done away.

When I was a child, I spake as a child, I understood as a child, I thought as a child: but when I became a man, I put away childish things.

For now we see through a glass, darkly; but then face to face: now I know in part; but then shall I know even as also I am known.

And now abideth faith, hope, charity, these three; but the greatest of these is charity."

Love is Patient: Being patient means we practice being in the present with ourselves and with others. We are not always rushing to get to the next thing or to the next place that we cut someone off. We build up a tolerance for waiting on God and on others. We become good listeners and we strive to put others ahead of ourselves even when it is uncomfortable.

Love is Kind: Kindness is about treating others the way we would like to be treated. Being kind means doing things with no expectation of a return or reward. Zero keeping scores of indiscretions. Being kind is about looking out for the welfare of others above your own. Being kind can also be a smile given to someone in the grocery store.

Love does not envy: Envy can be translated as jealousy. Love does not have negative feelings against another person because of their looks, gifts, friends, possessions, abilities, their popularity. Love celebrates instead of envying. Envy destroys relationships. We must choose to love; love is what it is.

Love does not boast: Boasting refers to bragging and seeking recognition, honor, or applause from others. A person who loves with God's love seeks to build up others. People with love in their hearts does not have to tell everyone about their own press report, they are content serving Jesus and giving HIM the credit.

Love is not proud: The King James Version notes that this means puffed up, prideful, arrogant, or conceited. Romans 12:3 notes, "For I say, through the grace given unto me, to every man that is among you, not to think of himself more highly than he ought to think; but to think soberly, according as God hath dealt to every man the measure of faith." Love is humble, does not consider itself better than others.

Love is not rude: Love does not dishonor others. Some people think it is cool or smart to offend others, but that is not what love is. We do it through the language we use, we do it through the tone of voice that we use, we do it when we take others for granted. But that is not what love is.

Love is not self-seeking: Keeps no record of wrong. Not easily angered. Love does not hold unforgiveness, old hurts, or hold grudges.

Love is not easily angered: Love has the capacity to be wronged and not retaliate.

Love keeps no record of wrongs: People who love deeply often love truth. They do not enjoy keeping up foolishness and holding grudges against others. They forgive others and wipe the slate clean, holding nothing over anyone's head.

Love Is

Honoring God

The greatest act of love is worship. Worship demands giving our whole selves. It is not a passive experience. To honor God, we love from a pure heart.

First Timothy 1:5 says, "Now the end of the commandment is charity out of a pure heart, and of a good conscience, and of faith unfeigned:" Real love honors God. It is a matter of the heart.

We honor God by serving: Matthew 20:28 states, "Even as the Son of man came not to be ministered unto, but to minister, and to give his life a ransom for many."

As believers, God counts us worthy to carry his name into all the world and to represent his Son, Jesus Christ well in the workplace, at home, and wherever our journeys may take us. God's needs are in the needs of people. We will never run out of opportunities to serve others. We serve God by serving people, that is the epitome of love.

Love is the primary nature of God. Born-again believers

receive His nature at the time of new birth, that nature comes with the desire to love, serve. Passion for purpose, worship, work, kingdom life.

Holy Spirit in you empowers us to walk in love.

Love is often tested by severe sufferings. Only true love can survive the sufferings of Christ. I believe we have not truly loved until that love has been tested and survived. Love without a cross is empty. Our ability to suffer long is related to our capacity to experience love.

Husbands and wives remain married because of their ability to endure self-sacrificing attitudes and behaviors. Wherever there is love, there is long-suffering, patience.

Love suffers long: One of the fruits of the Spirit is love and real love changes our hearts, our minds, and our entire beings. The presence of love in our lives will brings fullness if joy. We must let God fill our hearts and lives with HIS goodness, with HIS LOVE.

Love is the Chief of All Virtues

Matthew 5:48 states, "Be ye therefore perfect, even as your Father which is in heaven is perfect." Many people excel in different fields including sports and entertainment. They do well because of their love for and usage of the gifts and talents God has given them.

When we talk about love, we mean a much deeper

dimension of love, a virtue that is so paramount that it can be used to distinguish believers from all other people in the world. We are to be perfect not just in our talents but also in our love for God and others.

The love that God commands is a love that imitates His own. It is a perfect love that we are called to reflect and mirror, to be without blemish even as he is perfect.

We should carefully examine ourselves to see if this love resides in our hearts and if it is manifested in our lives. This passage in Scripture reveals how short we are in our love walk; it reveals our shortcomings. It demonstrates to us our lack of real love.

The gifts of God can be used without love, when that happens, their value is destroyed. The essence of love, Scripture tells us to seek the welfare of others. A person who reflects God's love is driven to give of himself for others, not use power for his own benefit.

Sometimes, we are more interested in supernatural power than supernatural love – that is shed abroad in our hearts. First Corinthians 13:2 notes, "And though I have the gift of prophecy, and understand all mysteries, and all knowledge; and though I have all faith, so that I could remove mountains, and have not charity, I am nothing."

Faith Works by Love

God is the only one who works on our behalf, we must have faith for God to act and answer our prayers for God is love. Really, we can say that love (God) is who answers our prayers and gives us our desires.

Therefore, when we are empty of love, our lives produce nothing. God never fails and because of that love never fails.

Jesus prioritized love as the mark of distinction for His disciples. John 13:31-35 states, "Therefore, when he was gone out, Jesus said, Now is the Son of man glorified, and God is glorified in him. If God be glorified in him, God shall also glorify him in himself, and shall straightway glorify him. Little children, yet a little while I am with you. Ye shall seek Me: and as I said unto the Jews, Whither I go, ye cannot come; so now I say to you. A new commandment I give unto you, That ye love one another; as I have loved you, that ye also love one another. By this shall all men know that ye are My disciples, if ye have love one to another."

First Thessalonians 5:21-22 notes, "Prove all things; hold fast that which is good. Abstain from all appearance of evil." Live a holy life and please the Lord. Make godly choices and avoid compromises that are ungodly. Distinguish yourselves from the world.

The root word of "distinction," is distinct, which means not alike and different in nature. It refers to a difference or contrast between similar things or people. For example, bananas and broccoli are both types of food, but one is considered a fruit and the other is a vegetable. Oranges and steak are types of food, but one is a fruit and the other is meat.

God identifies many distinctions in the world and throughout His Word. Here are a few you might be familiar with.

    Heaven and Earth
    Light and Dark
    Night and Day
    Male and Female
    Good and Evil
    Holy and Unholy
    Heaven and Hell
    Saved and Lost
    Jews and Gentiles
    Life and Death
    Righteous and Unrighteous
    Believers and Infidels
    Spirit and Flesh
    Godly and Ungodly

Titus 2:12-14 notes, "Teaching us that, denying ungodliness

and worldly lusts, we should live soberly, righteously, and godly, in this present world; Looking for that blessed hope, and the glorious appearing of the great God and our Saviour Jesus Christ; Who gave himself for us, that he might redeem us from all iniquity, and purify unto himself a peculiar people, zealous of good works."

First John 2:15 reminds us to abstain from loving the things in the world, "Love not the world, neither the things that are in the world. If any man love the world, the love of the Father is not in him."

God expects our attitudes, character and speech to be distinctly different from the world. Ephesians 4:29-32 states, "Let no corrupt communication proceed out of your mouth, but that which is good to the use of edifying, that it may minister grace unto the hearers. And grieve not the holy Spirit of God, whereby ye are sealed unto the day of redemption. Let all bitterness, and wrath, and anger, and clamour, and evil speaking, be put away from you, with all malice: And be ye kind one to another, tenderhearted, forgiving one another, even as God for Christ's sake hath forgiven you."

Love Lessons Learned from Daniel White, Jr.

In this chapter, I want to share some of the lessons I learned about love from my husband.

He was not argumentative

His refusal to be "fussy"? He kept peace in our relationship. I know there were times he wanted to express his feelings. Now I know for peace's sake, for the sake of love he refused to say anything negative. Wow! What a man.

Romans 12:18 exhorts us, "If it be possible, as much as lieth in you, live peaceably with all men." What does this speak to you in your relationships?

We always knew we were with the right person

I had a deep knowing in my heart he was God's best for me. He was a life partner. I didn't want to be without, who brought out the best in me. We fit like peas in a pod. He made me feel secure at all times. I trusted him. No doubt.

In what way does your relationship(s) challenge you. Who brings out the best in you and what is different about you because of the people in your life?

I learned how to love people

Danny was a God-given people's person. I was not! To be married to a person with opposite personalities is challenging in marriage. My then husband thought it was normal to bring an entire baseball team home for drinks and fellowship after a game was truly mind disturbing for me. I had to learn to accept his way of loving people if I wanted to stay married to him and the Lord blessed me to do so.

Colossians 1:8 tells us, "Who also declared unto us your love in the Spirit."

Because of love for one another, believers can have an impact that extends to neighbors, family and friends.

I learned that much of the love of Jesus can be shown in a loving relationship

God's gifts show up from love, that's so amazing to me. Forgiveness, kindness, patience, soft answers, love that wants what's best for someone else, no envy, no jealousy. Our heavenly Father teaches us to love as He loves in our relationships. Thank God Danny was patient with me.

First Corinthians 13:4-8 tells us, "Charity suffereth long, and is kind; charity envieth not; charity vaunteth not itself, is not puffed up, Doth not behave itself unseemly, seeketh not her own, is not easily provoked, thinketh no evil; Rejoiceth not in iniquity, but rejoiceth in the truth; Beareth all things, believeth all things, hopeth all things, endureth all things. Charity never faileth: but whether there be prophecies, they shall fail; whether there be tongues, they shall cease; whether there be knowledge, it shall vanish away."

What does 1 Corinthians 13:4-8 mean to you?

I learned that love is not confined to sexuality

Love is not dependent on good feelings but rather on a consistent and courageous decision to extend oneself for the well-being of another. That commitment then produces good feelings, not the other way around.

I learned a lot about Danny in the forty plus years we were married

Thank you for allowing me to encourage you. The Word of God teaches that marriage is honorable. Just as you love God more than anyone or anything, you love your spouse more than any other person. Just as you can be vulnerable and intimate in your relationship with God, you are to share an intimacy and vulnerability with your spouse that you should not share with anyone else. Because marriage should be a clear picture of our relationship with God. It is a symbol of Christ and the church. A marriage under God should teach couples how God relates to HIS church.

I learned to love intentionally

I learned to be happy with my decision to be married to him.

I intentionally decided to make him happy, to be the best wife, to spend a lifetime together, worshiping together, playing together, loving together, raising children together, solving problems together, praying together, staying together. "Love is what it is"—Together!

A Holy Nation in An Earthen Vessel by Evelyn B. Williams

When I speak of a Holy Nation, I do hope you understand,
I speak of a nationality of people, In the life of a God-sent man.
Yes! A Holy Vessel, In This Earthly Land.
Was the heart of Bishop Daniel White, Which will forever reign.

When God made these earthen vessels, with His own hands,
Dr. Daniel White was included, to be a great leader who would stand.
He chose to follow the Master: And go all the way.
Never to take down, no matter what people say.
His personality was an anointed one,
When you was right or when you was wrong,
He'd tell you—"Love is what it is." Get right and be strong.
The truth he never withheld; He was a Holy Nation in An Earthen Vessel.

Let's talk about this Holy Nation that was in his life.
It included foreigners, black and white, Color, he did not see.

The love of God in his heart was for humanity.
This precious love he possessed was not for sale,
He was a Holy Nation in An Earthen Vessel.

We know our body is the temple for the Holy Spirit to live in,
This is what Dr. White possessed and labored so hard
To get sinners saved from sin.
This job he did well. He's a Holy Nation in an Earthen Vessel.

When he sang, it truly blessed your soul,
You forgot about yourself as the Holy Ghost took control.
In your spirit you began to rejoice, just from hearing Dr. White's voice.
The load you thought you could not bear, Is no longer there.
Joy comes in and oh! how we rejoice, just from hearing Dr. White's voice.
There's no-one to fulfill his place,
The love he shared with others was God's amazing grace.
It spread through cities, states and communities, his personality did excel,
He's God's Holy Nation in An Earthen Vessel.

Don't you know that all Dr. White's children are not on the roll here!
Church, he has children everywhere.

Love and Worship Center just can't contain them all,

He would pick up and encourage anybody no matter where you fall.

I could never close this poem, it would be incomplete,

If I didn't include his lovely, devoted, God-anointed wife—apostle Shirley!

Chosen by God to be his helpmate, Laboring in love together,

Accomplishing the work that he did predestinate.

Bishop White's portion is done; What a beautiful race he did run,

And on Sunday morning his heavenly Father said, "Son, come on home."

You've been obedient, faithful, loving waters flowing from you—

More than anyone can tell you was my "Holy Nation, My Holy Earthen Vessel."

Frequently Asked Questions About Love

How can I know that God really loves me?

John 3:16 is how you know God loves you. He gave His only Son, Jesus Christ, so everyone who believes in Him will not perish but have eternal life. God sent His Son into the world not to judge the world, but to save the world. And because Jesus came and died, we are able to live and tell everyone else about him.

Ephesians 3:18-19 states, "May be able to comprehend with all saints what is the breadth, and length, and depth, and height; And to know the love of Christ, which passeth knowledge, that ye might be filled with all the fulness of God."

The more you get to know God through his Word and through his people, the more you will begin to see how inexhaustible His love is for you. One of the most powerful ways you can learn more about the love of God is by reading His Word daily.

What if I have no desire to love other people?

In John 13:34, the apostle writes, "A new commandment I

give unto you, That ye love one another; as I have loved you, that ye also love one another."

First John 2:9 states, "He that saith he is in the light, and hateth his brother, is in darkness even until now."

John 13:35 notes, "By this shall all men know that ye are My disciples, if ye have love one to another."

First John 4:12 tells us, "No man hath seen God at any time. If we love one another, God dwelleth in us, and his love is perfected in us."

Because of my selfish nature which I received from my birth from my Indian bloodline, I didn't know that you could love others like Christ loves us. However, after receiving the baptism of the Holy Spirit, I realized that having the love of God in your heart allows you to really love your enemies and to bless those who curse you. If we love each other, we show the world God lives in us, and that His love is stronger than anything else we could experience.

Why are we confused about God's love towards us?

I believe we desire to accept His love, but we wrongly understand it,

Many people believe in a "God of love", but according to their definition of love. Hopefully we all come to the full knowledge that He loves us with HIS Everlasting love.

In my favorite Psalm, Psalm 136, the psalmist repeats these words over and over again, "his mercy endures forever." Many believe that a loving God would not condemn anyone to hell. But let's not accept this distorted view of God and take his genuine love for us for weakness.

What is meant by God is love?

Because love is at the core of God's character.

God is the essence of love. The bible describes love as patient, kind, does not envy, does not boast, not proud, it is not rude, it is not self-seeking, it is not easily angered, it keeps no record of wrongs.

This is how the Bible describes God: All of God's attributes are in perfect harmony. Everything God does is loving. God is the perfect example of true love.

Jesus as our personal savior, God has given Him and those who receive Him the ability to love as He does, through the power of the Holy Spirit.

The Life of the Late Bishop Daniel White, Jr.

"A Melody of Love Divine"

Daniel White Jr. was born on April 27, 1934, to Daniel and Tempie White in the small community of James City, North Carolina. Daniel and his nine siblings, James, Louise, William, Tobias, Harriet, Rebecca, Dollie, Cherry, and Nancy had a humble start in life but were gifted with talents, wisdom, style and charisma. Daniel loved his family dearly with two siblings remaining as of the writing of this book, his sisters, Rebecca White Credle and Cherry White Tripp (Milton).

At the age of 17, Daniel enlisted in the United States Air Force and was stationed at Lackland Air Force Base in San Antonio, Texas. After training and reassignment and after several years of dedicated service, Daniel was honorably discharged in 1960. Soon after, Daniel took up civilian employment in Brooklyn, New York, with the assistance of his brother, Tobias. In Brooklyn, Daniel became a prolific gospel music singer, and pretty soon, became a member of St. Paul Disciple Church where he met the then Shirley L. Croom.

Daniel White, Jr. was united in holy matrimony to Shirley L.

Croom in Brooklyn, New York. From this union came four children, Daniel Alonzo, Sheila Adele, Temolynn Gladine, and Mark Anthony (Deceased, 2020), and their families, Leonard Anthony Martin (Sheila), Bobby Wintons Sr. (Temolynn), Meriqua Dixon (Daniel), and Stephanie Tillman (Mark). Daniel is also the grandfather to 18 grandchildren: Keeke Danielle, Meriqua Danni, Daniel IV, Duran, Tsciena, Danari (Jeremy), Danita, Dana, Daniqua, Jathan, Layfee, Danyel, Danyelle, Raevyn (Wade), Bobby Jr. Talia, Salome, and Mark Stephen as well as great-grandfather to nine great grandchildren.

Early in their marriage, the then young couple established a firm foundation as a result of their belief in God and His institution of marriage. In addition to grooming their own children, Daniel and Shirley became spiritual parents to countless souls throughout their over 42 years of marriage. Much of their time in Christian ministry has been spent counseling couples.

While in New Bern, NC, Daniel hosted a gospel television show that featured local Christian talent from the tri-county area called "Sunday Morning with Rev. Daniel White". Daniel served as a member of his family's church Mt. Shiloh Missionary Baptist Church for several years. He later attended the Undenominational Pentecostal Holiness Church where he was ordained and served as the associate pastor under the Late Dr. Willie Grant.

Moving to Apalachicola, Florida in 1978, Rev. White became pastor to 10 members of the Holiness Church of the Living God, Inc., in 1979. He was later ordained as a Bishop and became the third Presiding Bishop of the church, and under his leadership the membership grew. Because he was a man of love, preached and lived a message of love, the church came to be known as the Love Center. Bishop White later became the General Overseer of the Love Center Ministries, and the name of the church was officially named The Love Center and the "Love is what it is" theme was attached forever. Due to his dedication and years of labor, he received an Honorary Doctor of Divinity degree from the Undenominational Bible Institute of James City, North Carolina. Bishop White served the community of Apalachicola and surrounding cities as a spiritual leader for 23 years.

In 1999, Bishop White's gift of song was captured in his only album recording titled, "The Songbird of the South." Three years after his demise, Apostle Shirley C. White, Daniel White, Jr's widower, birthed the Love Center Ministries Worldwide, Network of Churches, Inc., where she continues to write Bishop's story and carry out his legacy in love. Apostle White serves as a Pastor to Pastors with the same love, care, and integrity.

About Apostle Shirley C. White

Shirley Croom White, an apostle of Christ Jesus by the command of God our Savior and of Christ Jesus our hope (1 Timothy 1:1), is the founder of the Love Center Church Inc., the General Overseer of Love Center Ministry Worldwide: Network of Churches Inc. and serves as the Dean of Love Center School of Ministry. Apostle White holds a Doctor of Divinity from the Undenominational Bible Institute of New Bern, North Carolina and is a certified Christian counselor. She has received countless awards and recognitions from over fifty years of ministry. She is the widower of the late Bishop Daniel White, Jr., whom she was married to for 44 years, and is a mother to four children, grandmother to 18 grandchildren, and great-grandmother to nine great-grandchildren.

A trailblazer and trendsetter, who focuses her attention on ministry training as a five-fold ministry leader. She provides counseling for pastors of growing congregations and is a self-published author, who continues to pen her life's work as a visionary leader who is concerned about the spiritual state of humankind and future generations. Her passion for helping others allows her to blend healthy living and biblical principles that encourage, motivate and inspire a holistic lifestyle. Apostle White, like Apostle John in 3 John 2 prays that the body of Christ may succeed, prosper and be in good health, just as our soul prospers.

Staying relevant in a changing world, Apostle White, fully embraces her role as a spiritual parent in God's kingdom and accepts the responsibility that comes with this generation and today's society. As a role model, apostle advocates for spiritually healthy families.

www.ingramcontent.com/pod-product-compliance
Lightning Source LLC
Chambersburg PA
CBHW062040120526
44592CB00035B/1725